FOCUS ON
ELEMENTARY
PHYSICS

3rd Edition

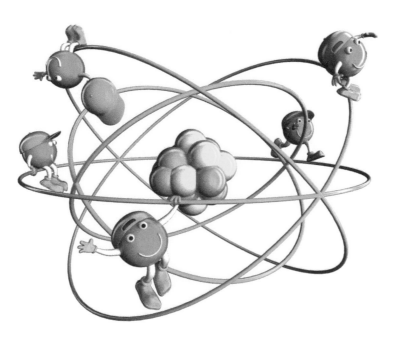

Rebecca W. Keller, PhD

Real Science-4-Kids

Illustrations: Janet Moneymaker

Focus On Elementary Physics Student Textbook—3rd Edition (softcover)
ISBN 978-1-941181-42-3

Published by Gravitas Publications Inc.
www.gravitaspublications.com
www.realscience4kids.com

Contents

◇◇◇

CHAPTER 1	**WHAT IS PHYSICS?**	**1**
1.1	Introduction	2
1.2	History of Physics	3
1.3	Modern Physics	5
1.4	Everyday Physics	6
1.5	Summary	6
1.6	Some Things to Think About	7
CHAPTER 2	**PHYSICIST'S TOOLBOX**	**8**
2.1	Introduction	9
2.2	Brief History	9
2.3	Basic Physics Tools	11
2.4	Advanced Physics Tools	11
2.5	Computers and Robotics	13
2.6	Summary	14
2.7	Some Things to Think About	14
CHAPTER 3	**PUSH AND PULL**	**16**
3.1	Up the Hill	17
3.2	Force	18
3.3	Work	19
3.4	Energy	21
3.5	Summary	22
3.6	Some Things to Think About	22
CHAPTER 4	**TYPES OF ENERGY**	**23**
4.1	Stored Energy	24
4.2	Types of Stored Energy	25
4.3	Releasing Stored Energy	26
4.4	Moving Energy	27
4.5	Summary	28
4.6	Some Things to Think About	28

CHAPTER 5 SAVING ENERGY   30

   5.1   Energy to Energy   31
   5.2   Energy We Use   32
   5.3   Energy We Waste   34
   5.4   Finding Energy   35
   5.5   Summary   37
   5.6   Some Things to Think About   37

CHAPTER 6 WHEN THINGS MOVE   38

   6.1   Moving Objects   39
   6.2   Keeping Objects in Motion   39
   6.3   Marbles and Bowling Balls   41
   6.4   Friction   42
   6.5   Summary   43
   6.6   Some Things to Think About   44

CHAPTER 7 LINEAR MOTION   45

   7.1   Introduction   46
   7.2   How Far?   46
   7.3   Average Speed   48
   7.4   Acceleration   49
   7.5   Summary   50
   7.6   Some Things to Think About   50

CHAPTER 8 NONLINEAR MOTION   52

   8.1   Introduction   53
   8.2   Throwing a Ball   53
   8.3   Riding a Bike   54
   8.4   Easy and Hard Gears   56
   8.5   Summary   59
   8.6   Some Things to Think About   59

CHAPTER 9 ENERGY OF ATOMS
AND MOLECULES   61

   9.1   Atoms and Energy   62
   9.2   Energy for Cars   64
   9.3   Energy in Food   65
   9.4   Batteries   66
   9.5   Summary   67
   9.6   Some Things to Think About   67

CHAPTER 10 ELECTRICITY   68

10.1	Introduction	69
10.2	Electrons	69
10.3	Electrons and Charge	71
10.4	Electrons and Force	72
10.5	Summary	73
10.6	Some Things to Think About	74

CHAPTER 11 MOVING ELECTRONS   75

11.1	Introduction	76
11.2	Electrons in Metals	77
11.3	Electrons in Other Materials	79
11.4	Summary	81
11.5	Some Things to Think About	81

CHAPTER 12 MAGNETS   82

12.1	Introduction	83
12.2	Magnetic Poles	84
12.3	Magnets and Force	88
12.4	Summary	89
12.5	Some Things to Think About	89

GLOSSARY/INDEX   90

Chapter 1 What Is Physics?

1.1	Introduction	2
1.2	History of Physics	3
1.3	Modern Physics	5
1.4	Everyday Physics	6
1.5	Summary	6
1.6	Some Things to Think About	7

1.1 Introduction

In this book we will take a look at the building block of science called physics.

Have you ever thrown a ball up in the air? Did you notice the ball when it left your hand? What did it do? Did it go up? Did it come back down? Unless it gets stuck in a tree or picked up by a big bird, a ball that is thrown up into the air will always come back down.

Have you ever tried to throw a ball really far or really high? Have you ever watched how far or how high the ball goes? Have you ever noticed that it's harder to throw a heavy ball than it is to throw a light ball? Have you ever noticed that it's almost impossible to throw a feather?

Physics is the branch of science that explores how far or how high a ball might go or how heavy it needs to be so that it can be thrown. Scientists who study physics are called physicists.

1.2 History of Physics

Physics is about studying the way things behave and then figuring out the rules those things follow to make them behave that way. Physicists don't make the rules, but they discover the rules by watching how the world works.

Aristotle studied motion, but it was Galileo Galilei, an Italian astronomer, who used physics to understand how things move.

Galileo is known for a famous experiment where he dropped two balls off a building to see what would happen. He used a heavy ball and a light ball. To everyone's surprise, he found out that they both hit the ground at the same time!

Physicists also use math to figure out the rules. Isaac Newton was a great scientist and mathematician who figured out many important rules of physics. By using math, Newton figured out exactly why the balls Galileo dropped hit the ground at the same time. Math is an essential part of physics and helps us understand the rules of physics.

1.3 Modern Physics

Did you know that balls will follow the same rules no matter where you are on the Earth? You can be in the frozen Arctic, and if you drop two balls, they will fall in exactly the same way. You can be in a desert, at the beach, or on a boat, and if you drop two balls, they will fall in exactly the same

way. No matter where you are on Earth, a ball will always follow the rules of physics!

How balls behave when dropped is explained by the rule "what goes up - comes down" which is a rule about gravity. Gravity is what makes the balls come back down.

Gravity is also what keeps you from flying off the surface of the Earth. Balls, toys, cars, houses, and even birds obey the rules of gravity.

1.4 Everyday Physics

Every day, physics is happening all around you. In the same way that you learn chemistry and biology, to learn physics you need to make observations. When you are looking at something with your eyes, you are making an observation. Making good observations is the first and most important step when you are trying to understand physics.

When you make an observation, try to notice everything you can about what you are observing. If you are at the movie theater getting popcorn, try noticing the popcorn machine. Where does the popcorn go in? Where does it come out? What is moving on the machine? What is staying still? Notice the popcorn when it comes out. Is it hot or is it cold? These kinds of observations are important if you want to think like a scientist.

1.5 Summary

● Physics is about studying the way things behave and then figuring out the rules those things follow that make them behave that way.

- Objects, like balls, planes, and birds, always obey the rules of physics.

- The rules of physics are true no matter where you are on the Earth.

- Physicists don't make the rules, they discover the rules.

- To think like a scientist, you must make good observations.

1.6 Some Things to Think About

- Go outside and throw a ball. Now throw a feather. How would you explain what happens?

- What do you think you could learn by dropping two balls off a tower?

- What do you think would happen if you were playing a ball game and the ball did not have to follow any rules of physics?

- The next time you go somewhere in a car, observe everything you can about the car and how the different parts work. Make a list!

Chapter 2 Physicist's Toolbox

2.1   Introduction   9

2.2   Brief History   9

2.3   Basic Physics Tools   11

2.4   Advanced Physics Tools   11

2.5   Computers and Robotics   13

2.6   Summary   14

2.7   Some
       Things to
       Think About   14

2.1 Introduction

How do you study what happens when you throw a ball in the air? How do you find out why a marble rolls? How do you measure heat and what is happening when you rub your hands together and they get warm?

Physicists study things like motion, heat, energy, and power. Since these things are sometimes hard to see and understand, physicists use tools that help them measure, map, and record how the world around them works.

2.2 Brief History

Physics is considered by some scholars to be the oldest and most basic science. Ancient philosophers thought a great deal about how the world works. One of these early philosophers was Thales of Miletus (625–545 B.C.E.). Thales was born in Greece, and he traveled to Egypt where he learned about geometry and astronomy.

THALES 625-545 BCE

IBN AL HAYTHAM
965-1040 CE

Greece was not the only place where philosophers were trying to understand how the world works. Ancient scholars in the Middle East, India, and China were all thinking about how the world works. The Muslim philosopher Ibn al-Haytham studied light and how light rays travel.

Omar Khayyam was a Persian scientist who accurately calculated the length of a year.

OMAR KHAYYAM
1048-1131 CE

SHEN KUO
1031-1095 CE

In China Shen Kuo was the first to describe the magnetic needle compass.

2.3 Basic Physics Tools

Physicists study the world by measuring, mapping, and monitoring how things work. Physicists want to know things like how far away something is or how long it takes something to go from point A to point B. Physicists need to know details, and to find those details physicists measure distances, times, weights, and temperatures. Some of the basic tools physicists use are timers, rulers, balances, and thermometers.

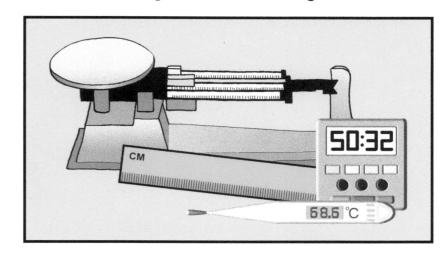

2.4 Advanced Physics

Physics covers a broad range of specialized subjects. Because there are so many subjects, there are many different kinds of tools.

Physicists who study sound might use a sound meter to measure high and low sounds.

Physicists who study the properties of objects and materials might use different dynamic testing machines to find out more about what these things are like.

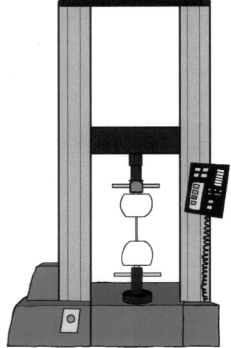

Some physicists study how objects go from hot to cold and might use a thermal imager to observe small changes in temperature.

Physicists who study electricity might use an oscilloscope to measure electrical waves.

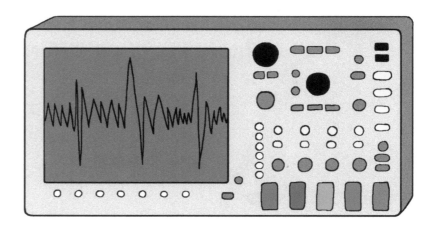

2.5 Computers and Robotics

Most advanced tools have computers inside or connect to a computer. In physics, computers are a very valuable tool. Computers can be programmed to collect large amounts of data. Computers can also be programmed to do complicated calculations or keep track of small distances.

Some high-level physics experiments use robots to move delicate instruments or record important information. Both computers and robotics have helped physicists learn more about how the world works.

2.6 Summary

- Physicists use a variety of basic tools and advanced tools (instruments) to do experiments.

- Many early philosophers from Greece, the Middle East, India, and China thought about how things work.

- Physicists use basic tools like rulers, timers, balances, and thermometers.

- Physicists use advanced tools (instruments) to measure movement, temperatures, sound, and electricity.

- Computers and robots help physicists make different kinds of measurements, collect large amounts of data, and do complicated calculations, among many other tasks.

2.7 Some Things to Think About

- Why do your hands get warm when you rub them together?

- Which ancient philosopher would you like to learn more about?

    Aristotle

    Thales

    Shen Kuo

    Omar Khayyam

    Ibn al Haytham

● What are some basic physics tools you have used?

● Which advanced physics tool have you used or seen used?

    oscilloscope

    thermal imager

    sound meter

    dynamic testing machine

    some other tool

● What are some tasks robots might do for scientists?

Chapter 3 Push and Pull

3.1   Up the Hill   17

3.2   Force   18

3.3   Work   19

3.4   Energy   21

3.5   Summary   22

3.6 Some Things to Think About   22

3.1 Up the Hill

What do you think would happen if you tried to take your baby sister up a hill in a wagon? You might start on flat ground at the bottom of the hill. First, you might grab the handle of the wagon, and as you did so, you might feel the wagon pull against you. You might think that the wagon with your sister in it is heavy.

Then, to get the wagon moving by pulling on it, you might need to use all of the strength in your arms and legs.

Once the wagon is moving on flat ground, you might find that it is easy to roll your sister along and that you don't have to use as many muscles. But, as you get to the bottom of the hill, you might need to use all your muscles again to pull the wagon uphill.

When you reach the top of the hill, you might discover that you are completely out of breath and a little tired. You might say that you used all your energy to do the work you needed to do to get your sister up the hill. And a physicist would say you are exactly right!

When you pull your little sister up a hill in a wagon, you are doing work and you are using energy. In physics, work is what happens when force moves an object. Energy gives you the ability to do work. But what is force? And what is energy?

3.2 Force

When you are pulling the wagon up the hill, you are using a force. Force is any action that changes the location of an object. Because you are changing the location of the wagon (and your sister) you are using force.

Force is also any action that changes the shape of an object. If you were to squeeze a marshmallow, you would be using force. By squeezing a marshmallow, you are changing its shape with the force created by your hands.

Force is also any action that changes how fast or how slowly an object is moving. You may have experienced this kind of force if you ever tried to catch the same ball as your friend. If you were both looking at the ball and not where you were going, you might have run into each other. When that happens—WHAM!—the two of you collide, and you both stop moving. In this action you each

used force to stop the other from moving. You could probably feel the effects of the force stay with your head or knees for several hours!

Force is any action that changes the location of an object, the shape of an object, or how fast or slowly an object is moving.

3.3 Work

In the first section we saw that work happens when force moves an object. Work also happens when force changes the shape of an object or when force changes how fast or how slowly an object is moving.

How is work related to force? If you use more force are you doing more work? Maybe. Or if you are doing more work, are you using more force? Yes!

Imagine that instead of one little sister, you have two. And imagine trying to pull both little sisters up the hill in the wagon.

It will take more muscles, more energy, and more effort to move two little sisters up the hill. In fact, if your little sisters were twins and weighed exactly the same amount, you would have to do twice the amount of work to get both of them up the hill.

The same is true for squeezing a marshmallow or running into your friend. If you squeeze the marshmallow more, you are doing more work. If you and your friend are running faster and generating more force, you are doing more work when you run into each other.

3.4 Energy

How do you get the energy for pulling your little sister up the hill in a wagon or for squeezing a marshmallow or for colliding with your friend? Where does the energy come from?

The energy for you to do all these things comes from your breakfast. When you eat breakfast, you are giving your body the energy it needs to do work. In physics, energy is something that gives something else the ability to do work. When you eat eggs or toast or cereal, your body takes the energy in the food and uses it in a way that helps your muscles move.

The food you eat for breakfast gives your muscles the ability to do work—like pulling a wagon full of sisters up a hill! And that's a lot of work.

3.5 Summary

● A force is any action that changes the location of an object or the shape of an object or how fast or slowly an object is moving.

● Work is what happens when a force moves an object.

● Energy is something that gives something else the ability to do work.

3.6 Some Things to Think About

● If you are pedaling a bicycle, do you think you are doing work? Are you using energy?

● If you pick up a puppy, do you think you are using force? If you use a spoon to make your ice cream mushy, do you think you are using force? If you throw a ball, do you think you are using force?

● Imagine that you throw a ball twice. The second time you throw it, the ball goes twice as far. Do you think you did different amounts of work each time you threw the ball?

● What do you like to eat for breakfast when you need lots of energy for the morning?

   eggs, sausage, pancakes, French toast, cereal and milk, ice cream, something else

Chapter 4 Types of Energy

4.1   Stored Energy   24

4.2   Types of Stored Energy   25

4.3   Releasing Stored Energy   26

4.4   Moving Energy   27

4.5   Summary   28

4.6   Some
        Things
        to Think
        About   28

4.1 Stored Energy

Recall from the last chapter that energy is something that gives something else the ability to do work. We saw how the food you eat for breakfast gives you the ability to move your muscles, which allows you to pull your little sister up a hill.

The food you eat for breakfast is a type of stored energy. Stored energy is energy that has not been used. A box of cereal may not look like it is full of energy, but in fact it has lots of energy molecules.

These energy molecules are called carbohydrates. When your body needs energy, it will break down the carbohydrate molecules so they can be used for moving muscles or walking to the store.

4.2 Types of Stored Energy

There are different types of stored energy. Have you ever taken a rubber band and stretched it across your finger and thumb? What happens when you release your thumb, letting the rubber band go? It flies through the air. There is stored energy in a rubber band.

But can you use this stored energy for breakfast? NO! You wouldn't eat rubber bands for breakfast!

A rubber band has a different type of stored energy than your breakfast cereal.

Breakfast cereal has chemical stored energy. Chemical stored energy is energy that comes from chemicals and chemical reactions.

A rubber band has elastic stored energy. Elastic stored energy is energy that is found in materials that can stretch.

A book on a table has gravitational stored energy. It could do work if it were to fall to the ground and smash an egg.

Gravitational stored energy comes from objects that are elevated above the ground and can be pulled down by gravity.

4.3 Releasing Stored Energy

When you let a rubber band go from your thumb, you release the stored elastic energy and the rubber band flew through the air. When you eat cereal for breakfast, your body breaks down the carbohydrate molecules, releasing the stored chemical energy so your muscles can pull a wagon. If a book falls off a table and onto the floor, the stored gravitational energy of the book is released and can be used to break an egg.

When each of these types of stored energy is released, the energy does not disappear but is converted into moving energy. The rubber band moved, the wagon moved, and the book moved.

In order for stored energy to do work, it must first be released. The stored energy in the rubber band, the breakfast cereal, and the book were all released and changed into moving energy. But what is moving energy?

4.4 Moving Energy

Moving energy is the energy found in moving objects. There is only one type of moving energy, and physicists call this energy kinetic energy.

Kinetic energy can come from different types of stored energy, but only the energy of a moving object is called kinetic energy.

When you release the stored energy in a rubber band and it's sitting on the floor, it can no longer do any work unless it is picked up and stretched again. When the rubber band is sitting on the floor, all of the stored energy has been released, and all of the kinetic energy has been used. You might think that the energy is lost. However, none of the energy disappears, it just gets changed to a different type of energy.

4.5 Summary

● Stored energy is energy that has not been used yet.

● There are different types of stored energy. Breakfast cereal has chemical stored energy. A rubber band has elastic stored energy.

● When stored energy is released, it can be changed into kinetic energy—the energy of an object that is moving.

4.6 Some Things to Think About

● According to physics, energy is ...

● Do you think a book that is sitting on a table is doing work? Do you think it has stored energy?

● How can you tell when the stored energy in a stretched rubber band is released?

● Name some objects you have seen that had kinetic energy.

Chapter 5 Saving Energy

5.1 Energy to Energy 31

5.2 Energy We Use 32

5.3 Energy We Waste 34

5.4 Finding Energy 35

5.5 Summary 37

5.6 Some Things to Think About 37

5.1 Energy to Energy

In the last few chapters you learned how energy is used when a force does work. You also learned about different kinds of energy. You learned about chemical stored energy, elastic stored energy, and gravitational stored energy. You also learned about kinetic, or moving, energy.

You learned that when a stretched rubber band is released, it can no longer do any work. But the energy is not lost, it has just changed to a different type of energy.

For example, if you look carefully at your brother when he is riding a bicycle, you can observe different types of energy being used to generate different kinds of forces and work.

Your brother's body is using chemical energy from his breakfast to move his muscles. The muscles are using the chemical energy to move the pedals on the bike. The pedals on the bike are connected to a chain and a gear. As the chain and the gear move, the wheels move. The chain, gear, and wheels are all using mechanical energy to move the bike forward.

In this example, you can see how one type of energy is getting converted, or changed, into another type of energy. As we saw in Chapter 4, energy is only converted (or changed) into other types of energy. Energy is never created, and energy is never destroyed. It is only changed from one form to another.

5.2 Energy We Use

When your dad puts gas in the car, he is giving the car energy it can use. Your body can't use gasoline to move the pedals on a bicycle, but a car uses gasoline to run the motor. Likewise, a car cannot use

cereal to move its motor like you use cereal to give energy to your legs.

There are different forms of energy, and not all types of energy can be used in the same way.

Gasoline is one form of energy that is used to power things like cars and boats. Cereal and bread are another form of energy used to power things like human bodies. Batteries are yet another form of energy used to power things like flashlights and laptop computers.

When we "use" energy, we are converting one form of energy to another form of energy.

When you use batteries in a music player, the chemical energy in the batteries is converted to moving and sound energy in the music player.

Eventually the batteries run out. All the chemical energy is converted to moving and sound energy, and there is no more chemical energy in the batteries. This is how we "use" energy. We convert it from one form to another form.

5.3 Energy We Waste

Even though energy cannot be destroyed, it is possible to "waste" energy. You might have heard your dad telling you to turn off the lights after you leave a room. Or you might hear your mom tell you not to leave the door open in the middle of winter. They may have told you not to "waste" energy. But if energy cannot be destroyed, what does it mean to waste energy?

Energy is "wasted" when energy is excessively or unnecessarily converted from one form to another form.

If you are playing with your battery powered car, then you are converting one form of energy (chemical energy in the battery) to another form of energy (moving energy in the car). Because you are playing with the car, it is necessary to convert the chemical energy.

But if you walk away from the car, and you forget to turn it off, the battery is running but you are no longer playing with the car. Now you are "wasting" the energy in the battery because you are not using it to play with the car. When you go back to your car the next day, you discover it won't work anymore because the battery is "dead." All the chemical energy in the battery is gone. This is wasting energy. You didn't destroy the energy, you just unnecessarily converted it from chemical to moving energy when you didn't need to.

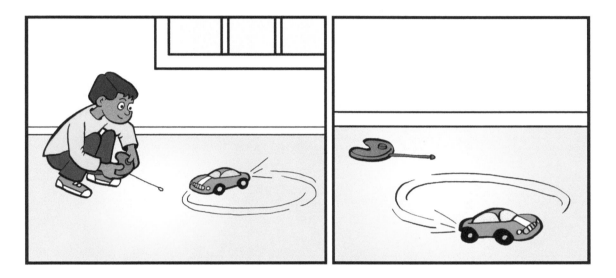

5.4 Finding Energy

We get much of our energy from the Earth. Gasoline, coal, and natural gas all come from inside the Earth. Nuclear energy also comes from the Earth in the form of plutonium. It is possible to get energy from moving water or wind, and we can also get energy from the Sun.

The food we eat comes from the Earth. We grow plants and raise animals to get food for our bodies. The plants get their energy from the Earth and also from the Sun.

Will we ever run out of energy? Yes and no. The energy we get from gasoline comes from fossils. There are only so many fossils in the ground, so it is possible that one day we will have used all the energy that is stored in fossils. When that happens, we will not have any more gasoline that comes from fossils to run our cars. This is also true with other forms of energy that come from fossils, such as coal or natural gas.

But if we remember that energy cannot be destroyed, only converted from one form to another, it may be possible to discover new ways to convert energy. Maybe there are new ways to convert the Sun's energy to chemical energy. Or maybe there are ways to get chemical energy from rocks. Or maybe there are ways to get electrical energy from grass or trees. Maybe you will be the next scientist who discovers a new way to convert energy into a form that can be used to power cars or boats or planes!

5.5 Summary

● Energy is neither created nor destroyed.

● Energy is converted from one form to another form.

● Energy is wasted by converting it from one form to another form excessively or unnecessarily.

● There may be new ways to convert energy to a form that can be used for fuel.

5.6 Some Things to Think About

● What examples can you think of where one type of energy is changed to another type of energy?

● Make a list of some objects you use that need batteries to work.

● What are some things people do that "waste" energy?

● What are some different ways that we can get energy we can use?

Chapter 6 When Things Move

6.1   Moving Objects   39

6.2   Keeping Objects in Motion   39

6.3   Marbles and Bowling Balls   41

6.4   Friction   42

6.5   Summary   43

6.6   Some Things
      to Think About   44

6.1 Moving Objects

A force is any action that changes the location or shape of an object or how fast or slowly an object is moving. You might think that forces also keep objects moving. This is what Aristotle thought. Aristotle was a philosopher in ancient Greece who studied how objects move. Aristotle thought that objects move because forces push on them from behind. However, 2,000 years later Galileo, an Italian physicist and astronomer, discovered that forces don't keep objects moving. Forces actually stop objects from moving. Forces can also change the direction of a moving object. But forces don't keep objects moving.

6.2 Keeping Objects in Motion

Galileo discovered that once an object is moving, it will keep moving unless it is stopped by a force. Forces can start an object moving or stop it, but forces do not keep an object moving. So, what keeps an object moving? An object keeps moving because of inertia. But what is inertia?

Have you ever been playing with your friends on the back porch when your mom called you to dinner? Maybe you didn't want to go to dinner. Maybe you wanted to keep playing. Maybe you even refused to stop playing and didn't go to dinner. That is inertia.

Inertia is when an object resists a change in motion. When you kept playing with your friend and did not want to change what you were doing to go to dinner, you had inertia. You didn't want to change your motion (playing) to a new motion (going to dinner). When you resisted going to dinner, you were like an object that doesn't want to stop moving. That is inertia.

Inertia also keeps objects still. When an object is moving, it wants to stay moving, and when an object is still, it wants to stay still. When an object does not want to change from moving to still or from still to moving, we say it has inertia.

6.3 Marbles and Bowling Balls

Everything has inertia. Bananas, oranges, bowling balls, and marbles all have inertia. You have inertia. If you are standing in the middle of your room refusing to put your pajamas on, that is inertia. If you are running down a hill and you can't stop, that is inertia. So whether you are moving or not moving, you have inertia. Whether you are tall or short, young or old, you have inertia. Everything that has mass has inertia. But what is mass?

In physics, inertia comes from a property called mass. Everything has inertia because everything has mass. Simply put, mass is how heavy something is. A heavy bowling ball has more inertia than a light marble. Because a bowling ball weighs more (has more mass) than a marble, it has more inertia.

Think about how hard it is to roll a bowling ball. Now think about how easy it is to roll a marble. It is harder to get

a bowling ball to move than it is to get a marble to move. Why? Because a bowling ball has more inertia. It is also harder to get a bowling ball to stop moving than it is to stop a marble. Why? Again, because a bowling ball has more inertia than a marble.

6.4 Friction

We said that objects don't stop moving unless a force makes them stop. Because everything has inertia, an object in motion will stay in motion.

But wait! If you roll a soccer ball on the soccer field, it will eventually stop even if another soccer player doesn't make it stop. Why? Why does a soccer ball stop moving even if no one is there to make it stop?

It stops moving because of friction. Remember, all objects will keep moving (because all objects have inertia) unless a force makes them stop moving. Everywhere on Earth, friction makes things stop moving. Friction is a force that stops objects from moving.

Friction can come from almost anything. The grass in the soccer field makes friction that stops the rolling soccer ball. If a ball is thrown into a swimming pool, the ball will eventually stop moving because of the friction created by the water. Even air creates friction. If a ball is thrown into the sky, it will eventually slow down and stop moving because of friction caused by the air.

6.5 Summary

- A force is any action that changes the location or shape of an object or how fast or slowly an object is moving.

- Forces make objects start to move, and forces also stop objects from moving. But forces do not keep objects moving.

- Inertia keeps objects still and keeps objects moving.

- Simply put, mass is how heavy something is.

- Friction is a force that will stop objects that are moving.

6.6 Some Things to Think About

● How do you think objects keep moving?

● How would you explain inertia in your own words?

● Which object has the most inertia (when it's not moving)?

    a marble

    a bowling ball

    an elephant

    a mouse

    an airplane

● What do you think happens in space? Is there friction?

Chapter 7 Linear Motion

7.1   Introduction   46

7.2   How Far?   46

7.3   Average Speed   48

7.4   Acceleration   49

7.5   Summary   50

7.6   Some Things
       to Think About   50

7.1 Introduction

In Chapter 4 we explored kinetic energy, or moving energy. In this chapter we are going to look at a specific kind of motion called linear motion. Linear motion is simply motion that occurs along a line. If you push a hockey puck straight in front of you, it has linear motion. If you throw a baseball straight into the catcher's mitt, it has linear motion.

7.2 How Far?

Did you know that everything is moving? Even objects you think are standing still are moving. Your house is moving and even mountains are moving! You can tell houses and mountains are moving because you can see the Sun shine on them in the morning and then stop shining on them at night. Your house and the mountains around you are moving because the Earth is moving as it spins around and around on its axis. The Earth is also moving around the Sun.

Physicists say that motion is relative. This means that we measure the motion of an object by comparing it to other objects. Physicists use the term speed to mean how fast an object moves. The speed of an object is *relative* to the objects surrounding it. For example, if a police officer pulls you over and hands you a speeding ticket, it is because you were moving too fast compared to him, the road, and the houses around him.

The speed of an object is the measure of how far it goes in a given time. If you start at your back porch and run to the back wall of your yard and it takes you three minutes, you ran that distance at a certain speed. But if your friend runs to the back wall of your yard and finishes the same distance in only one minute, then your friend ran faster than you did. A physicist would say your friend ran with more speed.

7.3 Average Speed

Physicists like to study details. If you ran to the back wall three times, a physicist would observe your speed the first time, the second time, and the third time you ran. The physicist would clock how fast you ran each time and would record three

separate times. The speed at which you ran might have been affected by different things. For instance, if you got more tired each time you ran, your speed might have been slower the second time you ran and even slower the third time.

Imagine that you want to know on average how fast you can run to the back wall of your yard. To find your average speed you would add all three of your times together and then divide by three. This would tell you on average how fast you ran.

Knowing your average speed is useful information. You might find out that on average you can run to the back wall in two minutes, but on days when you feel really good you can run this distance on average in less than two minutes. By recording your average speed each day and making notes about how you were feeling and other things such as what you had for breakfast, you can compare your good days and your bad days and learn about what helps you run faster.

7.4 Acceleration

Imagine that you are running to the back wall and suddenly your friend starts to run beside you. You might try to win the race, so you speed up! Then as you get near the end, you might start to get tired and have to slow down.

When you started to run faster, you changed your acceleration. In physics, acceleration is the change in speed of a moving object for a given time. For example, if you roll a marble down a ramp, you can watch it accelerate as it gets closer to the ground. The marble will start slowly and then gradually speed up. Depending on how long your ramp is, the marble might be moving very fast when it hits the ground. Because the marble speeds up as it travels down the ramp, physicists say it accelerates—changes its speed as it moves.

7.5 Summary

- Linear motion is the motion of an object in a straight line.

- Speed is how fast an object travels.

- Average speed is calculated by measuring the speed of an object several times, adding the speeds together, and dividing the total by the number of times the speed was measured.

- An object accelerates when it changes its speed while it is moving.

7.6 Some Things to Think About

- Do you think a car has linear motion? Why or why not?

- How far can you run in 2 minutes?
    - across the backyard
    - to the neighbors house
    - to the grocery store
    - to the next city
    - across your country
    - some other distance

● What do you think would be the most helpful to you if you want to be able to run faster?

  a good breakfast

  new shoes

  practicing every day

  running in a race

  something else

● How would you explain acceleration in your own words?

Chapter 8 Nonlinear Motion

8.1   Introduction   53

8.2   Throwing a Ball   53

8.3   Riding a Bike   54

8.4   Easy and Hard Gears   56

8.5   Summary   59

8.6   Some Things
       to Think
       About   59

A   B

8.1 Introduction

In the last chapter we saw how the speed of an object can be measured when it is moving in a straight line. We learned that movement in a straight line is called linear motion. In this chapter we are going to look at nonlinear motion, or what happens when an object is not moving in a straight line.

8.2 Throwing a Ball

What happens if you go outside and throw a ball across your backyard? The ball moves forward, relative to your position, and travels to the other side of the yard. In the last chapter, we discovered that this type of motion is called *linear motion.*

But the ball not only moves forward, it also moves up and down. The up and down motion forms a curved path. Because this path is curved and not straight, it is called nonlinear motion. Nonlinear motion is motion that does not follow a straight line.

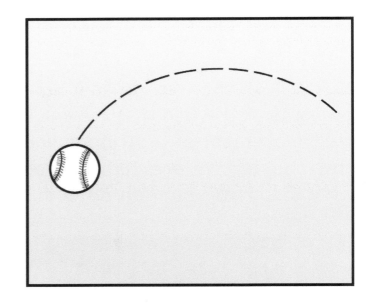

8.3 Riding a Bike

When you sit on a bike and push the pedals, you are using your legs to move you and your bike forward. If you are pedaling your bike and you look down at the frame of the bike, you will see that both you and the bike frame are moving forward in a straight line. This is an example of linear motion.

However, if you look below the bike frame and notice the wheels, you will see that the wheels are turning as you pedal. In physics, we call this type of motion nonlinear motion. The wheels are traveling in a circle, around the center hub. We could say the wheels are rotating. Also, because the wheels are traveling in an exact circle, they are moving with a special type of nonlinear motion called rotational motion.

One way to observe the rotational motion of a bike wheel is to put a blue dot on the rear wheel and prop the bike up so the rear wheel is off the ground. As the pedals are pushed, the rear wheel moves, and the blue dot travels in a circle. This makes it easy to see the rotational motion of the wheel.

Bicycle wheels, car wheels, motorcycle wheels, airplane propellers, and even CDs move with rotational motion. In the case of bicycles, cars, motorcycles, and airplanes, the rotational motion of the wheels and propellers is converted to linear motion as the vehicle moves forward. In the case of a CD spinning in a CD player or in a computer, the movement of the CD is not converted to linear motion but to sound. However, in all cases, the wheels, propellers, and CDs are moving with rotational motion. They are all moving in a circle.

8.4 Easy and Hard Gears

Have you ever used a bike to go fast on a flat street? And have you ever used a bike to climb slowly up a steep hill? If you have a bike with more than one gear, you probably used a hard gear to go fast on a flat street and an easy gear to climb up a hill.

On a bicycle, gears are simple machines that use rotational motion to make it easier to climb hills and go fast on flat streets.

If you look carefully at the pedals of a single gear bicycle, you will see that they are attached to a metal wheel that has teeth. If you look at the rear wheel, you will see another metal wheel with teeth. Each of these metal wheels with teeth is called a sprocket. A chain goes around both of the two sprockets, joining them together.

When you use the pedals to turn the front sprocket, the chain transfers this motion to the sprocket on the back wheel, turning the wheel and moving the bicycle forward.

The combination of front sprocket, back sprocket, and the chain joining them is called a gear.

If you look at a bike that has more than one gear, you will see that it has several different size sprockets on the front and several different size sprockets on the back. By combining different sizes of front and back sprockets, you can make the bike easier or harder to pedal.

If the front sprocket is much larger than the back sprocket, the gear is harder to pedal but makes the back wheel move very fast. On a flat surface this gear is used for speed.

If the front sprocket is smaller than the back sprocket, the gear is easier to pedal but moves the back wheel very slowly. Because the gear is easier to pedal, this gear can be used to climb hills.

By understanding how gears work, you can pick gears to help you go uphill with less effort and downhill faster!

8.5 Summary

- Nonlinear motion is motion of an object that moves in a curve or in a circle.

- Rotational motion is a type of nonlinear motion of an object that rotates or moves in a circle.

- Bicycles, cars, motorcycles, and airplane propellers use rotational motion of the wheel or propeller to move them forward.

- The gears on a bicycle use rotational motion. Different size sprockets are used to make a bike go faster or make it easier to climb hills.

8.6 Some Things to Think About

- What are some things you've seen that move with nonlinear motion?

- When you ride a bike, which parts of the bike are moving with nonlinear motion? Which parts are moving with linear motion?

  When you ride a bike, which parts of *you* are moving with nonlinear motion? Which parts of you are moving with linear motion?

● What is your favorite type of sport that uses a ball?

    basketball

    soccer

    American football

    rugby

    tennis

    baseball

    cricket

    ping pong

    lacrosse

    a different sport

● How would you explain in your own words how the gears on a bike work?

● Look around for more objects that have gears. What to these gears do?

    Do some objects have sprockets but not gears?

Chapter 9 Energy of Atoms and Molecules

9.1   Atoms and Energy   62

9.2   Energy for Cars   64

9.3   Energy in Food   65

9.4   Batteries   66

9.5   Summary   67

9.6   Some
      Things
      to Think
      About   67

9.1 Atoms and Energy

Every material object has mass. Simply put, mass is how heavy something is. A tree has mass. A football has mass. You have mass.

Recall from Chapter 6 that inertia is a force that keeps objects still and keeps objects moving. The more mass an object has, the more inertia it has. That is, the more mass an object has, the harder it is to start the object moving or to get the object to stop moving.

Every material object has mass because every object is made of atoms. Atoms are what make objects into objects. A tree is made of atoms. A fish is made of atoms. Your body is made of atoms.

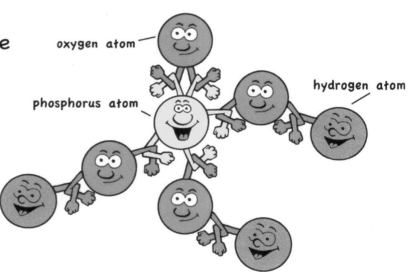

oxygen atom

phosphorus atom

hydrogen atom

Phosphoric Acid
A molecule

When two or more atoms are connected together, a molecule is formed. Phosphoric acid is a molecule made of the atoms oxygen, hydrogen, and phosphorus.

When molecules interact with other molecules or atoms, a chemical reaction takes place.

What happens when you add baking soda to vinegar? Bubbles start to form, and the baking soda turns to foam. This is a chemical reaction. It takes energy for a chemical reaction to take place.

Where did the baking soda and vinegar get the energy? The energy is inside the baking soda and vinegar molecules. This is called chemical energy. Atoms and molecules have stored chemical energy. When a chemical reaction occurs, the energy stored inside the molecules is released and used to do work. Work is done when a force moves an object or changes its shape.

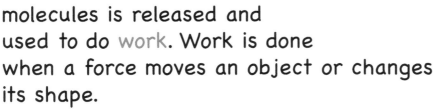

You can see the work being done if you put baking soda and vinegar together in a bottle and close the lid. The stored chemical energy of the baking soda and vinegar in the bottle will release, causing a chemical reaction.

The chemical reaction will make gas which will begin to press on the sides and top of the bottle and will put pressure on the lid. If there is enough energy used and enough gas created, the bottle might explode and the lid pop off! This is stored chemical energy being used to do work.

9.2 Energy for Cars

How does your car get energy for moving? Does your mom feed the car hamburgers? Or do your parents take it to a field and let it graze on the grass with the cows?

No! Your parents take your car to the gas station to fill the gas tank with gasoline.

Gasoline is a type of stored chemical energy used for fuel by cars, motorcycles, airplanes, and boats. The stored chemical energy in gasoline is released when your mom or dad starts the car. When the chemical energy is released, it can be used to move parts of the car so that the car's wheels can roll down the street.

9.3 Energy in Food

The cereal you eat for food is a type of stored energy. Foods, like potatoes, cereal, and bread, contain a type of stored chemical energy called carbohydrates.

Carbohydrates are special kinds of molecules that living things use for fuel. Sugar is a type of carbohydrate. Our bodies use lots of carbohydrates for energy.

The body breaks down carbohydrate molecules and uses the energy to move muscles, to make our heart beat, and even to think! It takes lots of energy to think, and eating carbohydrates is one way to give our bodies the fuel needed for thinking!

9.4 Batteries

Batteries are another type of stored chemical energy. What happens when you put batteries in a flashlight or in a game player?

Inside a battery are metals and chemicals. When the metals and chemicals come in contact with each other, a chemical reaction occurs. The chemical energy inside the battery is changed into electrical energy, and the electrical energy runs the flashlight or game player. We'll learn more about electrical energy in the next chapter.

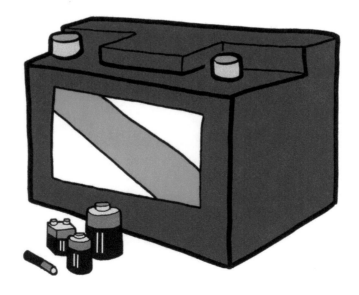

9.5 Summary

- Chemical energy comes from atoms and molecules and is released in chemical reactions.

- Gasoline is a type of stored chemical energy used by cars, boats, and motorcycles.

- Carbohydrates are a type of stored chemical energy in food and are used by living things for fuel.

- Batteries are a type of stored chemical energy used by flashlights and game players.

9.6 Some Things to Think About

- How would you describe a chemical reaction?

  If you mix baking soda and vinegar and a chemical reaction takes place, will you still have baking soda and vinegar? Why or why not?

- What do you think the world would be like if gasoline didn't have stored chemical energy?

- How do you think the stored energy in cereal is released by your body?

- Why do you think a flashlight stops working if you forget to turn the flashlight off?

Chapter 10 Electricity

10.1 Introduction   69

10.2 Electrons   69

10.3 Electrons and Charge   71

10.4 Electrons and Force   72

10.5 Summary   73

10.6 Some
      Things
      to Think
      About   74

10.1 Introduction

In Chapter 9 you learned about chemical energy. Recall that chemical energy is energy inside atoms and molecules. When a chemical reaction occurs, chemical energy is released from the atoms and molecules.

You also learned that sometimes chemical energy is converted into electrical energy. Batteries convert chemical energy into electrical energy. But exactly where does the electrical energy come from?

10.2 Electrons

Electricity, or electrical energy, comes from electrons. An electron is part of an atom.

Look at your body. Notice that your body has different parts. You have eyes for seeing, legs for walking, and arms for picking up objects. Inside your body you also have lots of parts. You have lungs for breathing, a stomach for digesting food, and a heart for pumping blood. You have many parts to your body, and each part does something different.

In a similar way, an atom has different parts. An atom has three main parts called protons, neutrons, and electrons. The protons and neutrons are in the center of the atom, and the electrons move around outside this center.

The electrons are what make atoms stick to each other to form molecules during a chemical reaction. In the following illustration of a carbon atom, the "arms" represent the electrons that are used by carbon to stick to other atoms. The yellow and blue balls inside the carbon atom represent the protons and neutrons.

The electrons of an atom can jump back and forth during a chemical reaction. That is, atoms can exchange electrons.

You can't give your arms to someone else when you meet them, but an atom can give part of itself (the electron) to another atom to form a chemical bond. It is the moving of these electrons that causes electrical energy. In metals, electrons jump from atom to atom all the time. Some metals have lots of electrons that jump from atom to atom.

10.3 Electrons and Charge

What happens when you rub a balloon in your mom's hair? If you pull the balloon away just slightly, your mom's hair will travel with the balloon. Physicists say that the balloon is charged. In this case, "charged" means that the balloon is attracted to the hair and the hair is attracted to the balloon. But why? Why does the balloon attract your mom's hair and the hair attract the balloon? What makes the balloon "charged?"

Electrons make the balloon charged. Electrons have a charge. That means that they have the ability to attract or repel other things that also have a charge. Protons have a charge but neutrons are neutral. Neutrons have no charge (that is why they are called neutrons, because they are neutral).

Physicists and chemists say that electrons are negatively charged and protons are positively charged. This is just one way to say that their charges are opposite. This is a "rule" that scientists follow so it is easier to talk about charges.

In physics, opposites attract. Positive charges attract negative charges, and negative charges attract positive charges. Therefore, protons attract electrons, and electrons attract protons because they have opposite charges.

When you rub a balloon in your mom's hair, electrons hop from your mom's hair to the balloon. Because there are now more electrons on the balloon and electrons have a negative charge, the balloon is negatively charged. Your mom's hair lost some electrons and now has more protons that have a positive charge, so her hair is positively charged. Because your mom's hair and the balloon are charged with opposite charges, they attract each other!

10.4 Electrons and Force

Forces cause things to move. This is true for large things, like wagons, and small things, like electrons. Electrical forces cause electrons to move.

Have you ever rubbed your feet on the carpet and then touched a door knob? If the air was dry enough, you probably felt the effects of electrical forces moving

electrons. You might have felt a small shock when —ZAP!— you touched the door knob. This is electrical force moving electrons.

10.5 Summary

- Electricity, or electrical energy, comes from electrons.

- Electrons are part of an atom. Atoms have protons, neutrons, and electrons.

- Electrons can move from atom to atom.

- Electrons are negatively charged. Protons are positively charged, and neutrons are neutral.

10.6 Some Things to Think About

● What is your favorite object that runs on chemical energy?

    Car

    Cell phone

    Computer

    Flashlight

    Radio

    Airplane

    Something else

● Do you think neutrons and protons can make electrical energy? Why or why not?

● If you rub a balloon in your hair, why will your hair stick to it?

    Can you think of something else you could rub in your hair to make your hair stick to it? Try it!

● Do you think it would take as much force to move an electron as it would to move a wagon? Why or why not?

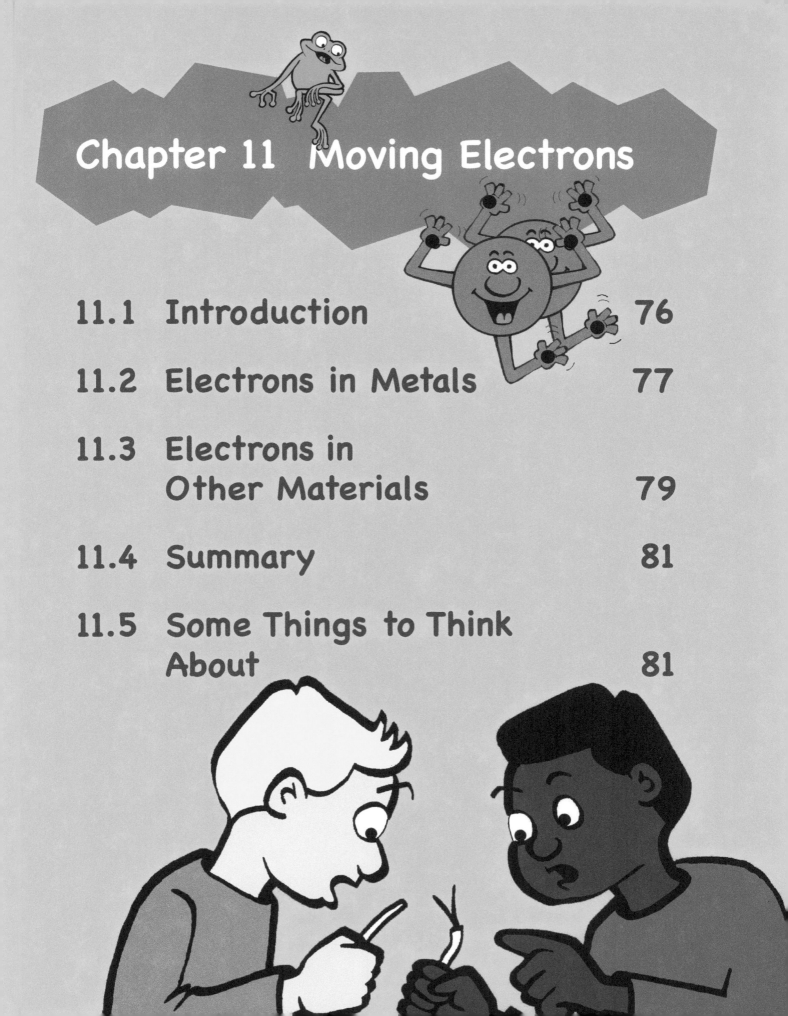

Chapter 11   Moving Electrons

11.1   Introduction   76

11.2   Electrons in Metals   77

11.3   Electrons in
       Other Materials   79

11.4   Summary   81

11.5   Some Things to Think
       About   81

11.1 Introduction

In Chapter 10 you learned how electrical energy comes from the movement of electrons. You learned that electrons can jump from atom to atom, or even from hair to balloons! You also learned that electrons are charged and that scientists say that electrons have a negative charge and protons have a positive charge.

Everything that is made of atoms has electrons. All material objects have electrons. Wooden tables have electrons. Marshmallows have electrons. Frogs have electrons.

Many kinds of materials will allow a small number of electrons to move through them. But only some types of materials allow lots of electrons to move through them. Scientists say that these types of materials conduct electricity. This means that lots of electrons can flow through them, like water flowing through a garden hose.

11.2 Electrons in Metals

If you look at a toaster, you notice that it is connected to a cable, and this cable is plugged into the wall. Inside the wall there is another cable that goes outside and connects to a big pole. This pole has cables on it that bring electricity into your house. In  some houses the cable in the wall goes to electrical cables that are buried under the ground instead of being on poles. In either case, the toaster needs to be plugged into the wall to get electricity in order to work.

This is also true for your computer (if it doesn't run on a battery). It is also true for your television set or video game player. All of these items need electrical energy to work. And all of these items are connected to wires or cables that are plugged into the cable in the wall that brings the electricity into your house.

If you open up one of the cables, you might see that it is made of metal wires. Copper metal is often at the center of most cables or wires because copper can conduct electricity. The reason copper can conduct electricity (allow electrons to flow) is because some of the electrons on the copper atoms are very loosely attached. That is, the electrons can easily jump from one atom to the next.

Copper atoms have lots of electrons. In the following illustration, the "arms" on each copper atom are replaced with dots to represent the electrons.

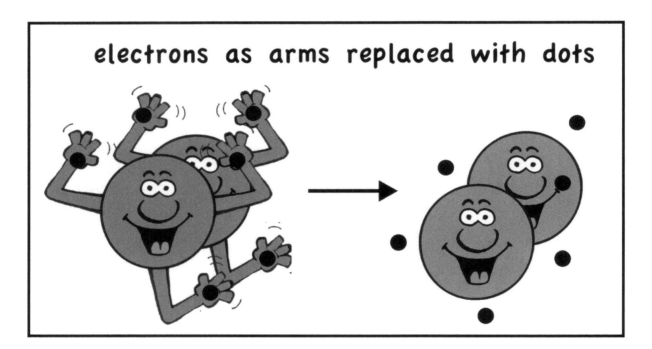

In a piece of copper metal, lots of copper atoms are next to each other. This means that there are lots of electrons free to hop around. This is why copper is a good conductor.

Just like water can flow through a garden hose because the water molecules are not attached to the hose, electrons can flow through a metal wire because the electrons are not tightly attached to the metal atoms.

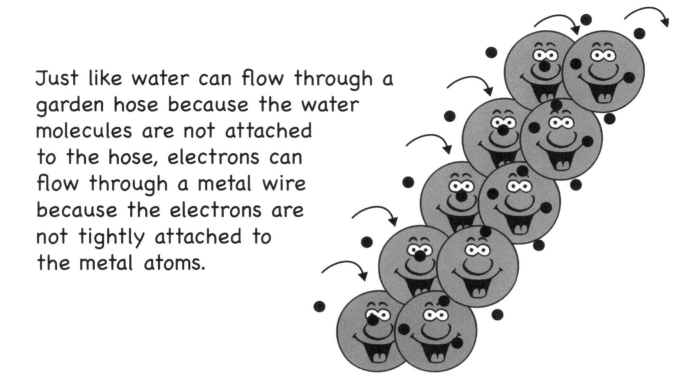

11.3 Electrons in Other Materials

You saw in the introduction that all materials have electrons. Marshmallows, teddy bears, wooden tables, and popcorn all have electrons. But these materials are not used for moving electrons. Scientists say that these materials do not conduct electricity. That is, they do not allow the electrons to hop from one atom to the next.

The electrons in materials that do not conduct electricity are more tightly held to the atoms. Because they can't hop from atom to atom, there is no flow of electrons through the materials.

Scientists call these materials insulators. If you look closely at the cable that connects your toaster to the wall, you will see that it is covered in plastic. Plastic is an insulator. Plastic does not allow electrons to move through it, so it does not conduct electricity.

Insulators keep the electrons from moving from wires to your hands. This is important because even though you are not made of metal, your body will conduct electricity! If you touch a wire used for moving electricity and it does not have a plastic covering, you could get a big shock! This is why

DON'T TOUCH THIS ONE. THE PLASTIC IS GONE AND ELECTRONS CAN MOVE TO YOUR HANDS AND SHOCK YOU.

it is always important to be careful not to touch electric wires or electric outlets. The amount of electricity that moves through the wires is too large for your body and can hurt you.

11.4 Summary

● Every material substance (everything that is made of atoms) has electrons.

● Metals are called conductors.

● Electrons move from atom to atom in a conductor much like water moves through a garden hose.

● Other materials, like plastic, are called insulators. Electrons do not move through these.

11.5 Some Things to Think About

● Wooden tables and marshmallows have electrons. Do you think they can conduct electricity? Why or why not?

● Why do you think a light bulb goes off when you move the switch to the "off" position?

● Why do you think it's important that some materials are insulators and others are not?

Chapter 12 Magnets

12.1 Introduction   83

12.2 Magnetic Poles   84

12.3 Magnets and Force   88

12.4 Summary   89

12.5 Some
      Things to
      Think About   89

12.1 Introduction

In Chapter 10 you learned that electrons have a negative charge and protons have a positive charge. Remember, this is just one way to say that the charges are opposite.

If you look around, you can see lots of different kinds of opposites. Black is the opposite of white. Wet is the opposite of dry. Dark is the opposite of light. North is the opposite of south. East is the opposite of west.

Sometimes opposites attract. In Chapter 10 you learned that positive charges attract negative charges—opposite charges will attract each other. This attraction creates the force that holds atoms together.

Some materials create attractive forces that aren't charged. A magnet is a type of material that will create an attractive force, but a magnet is not charged. Although a magnet is not charged, a magnet has opposite poles, and the opposite poles attract.

12.2 Magnetic Poles

All materials not only have electrons, but all the electrons are spinning. Magnets are usually made of nickel or iron. Some materials, like copper, don't make magnets. In metals that aren't magnetic, there are an equal number of electrons spinning. But in metals that are magnetic, like nickel or iron, there are an unequal number of electrons spinning. Because these metals have an unequal number of electrons spinning, they create magnetic poles.

One way to think about magnetic poles is to imagine a box full of marbles. Imagine that you have an equal number of marbles. Imagine also that each marble is half white and half black. To make it simple, imagine that you also gave all the marbles a "rule."

The rule is: "The marbles have to be balanced." So, for every marble with the black side facing forward, there must also be a marble with the black side facing backward. For every marble with the black side

facing upward, there must be a marble with the black side facing downward. This way the black and white colors on the marbles are balanced.

If you throw all the marbles into the box, there will be a mixture of marbles. Some of the marbles will have the black side facing up; some will have the black side facing down. Some marbles will have the black side facing forward and some backward. The marbles will be mixed, but because there is an equal number of marbles, all the directions the marbles are facing balance out.

Now imagine that you throw one more marble in the box. This marble has the black side facing up. But there isn't another marble to balance this one out. So what do the marbles do?

In a metal, this is what happens with the electrons. Because there is an extra electron on metal atoms, the spins are not balanced.

One way to get more balance is for all the marbles to line up in one direction. When the marbles do this, the effect of one extra marble is not so noticeable.

All the black sides face one way, and all the white sides face the other way. Since all the marbles are facing the same way, you could say that one side of the box is "white" and the other side is "black." In this way, the box has "opposite" sides."

In a metal, when the extra electron gets all the electrons spinning in the same direction, it is just like having all the marbles line up with the white sides pointing in one direction and the black sides pointing in the other direction. In a metal, this creates a magnetic pole.

Because the poles in a magnet are not charged, we don't call them "positive" and "negative." Instead we say "north" and "south." The north pole and the south pole are opposite and attract each other.

Sometimes magnets will have the letters "N" and "S" written on them. These letters mean "North" and "South."

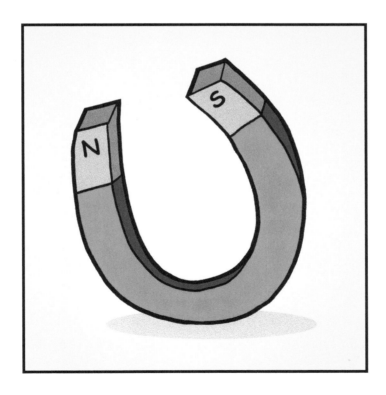

12.3 Magnets and Force

If you have played with magnets, you may have observed how one pole of a magnet will strongly attach to the opposite pole of another magnet. You also might have observed how the same poles of two magnets won't go together. No matter how hard you try to push them together, the same poles will not touch. If you hold the magnets in your hands, you can feel the force of the poles attracting each other or pushing each other away. This force is called a magnetic force.

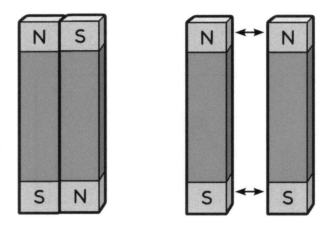

Magnetic forces are caused by the spinning electrons inside magnetic metals. The forces generated by magnets can be quite strong. Magnets can be used to lift cars or hold heavy equipment together. The Earth is also a huge magnet! If you travel north anywhere on the Earth, you'll end up at the North Pole. If you travel south anywhere on the Earth you'll end up at the South Pole. The North and South Poles are the ends of the magnet we live on called Earth!

12.4 Summary

- Only some metals, like nickel and iron, can be magnets.

- A magnet has opposite poles called a north pole and a south pole.

- The poles of a magnet are not charged.

- Magnetic force is caused by spinning electrons.

12.5 Some Things to Think About

- Make a list of some more things that are opposites.

- What do you think will happen if you put the north pole of one magnet next to the south pole of a second magnet?

- Make a list of some things that you use magnets for.

Glossary-Index

acceleration (ik-sel-uh-RAY-shun) • the change in speed of a moving object for a given time, 49

Aristotle (ER-uh-stah-tul) • [384-322 BCE] Greek philosopher; used physics to understand how things move, 4, 39

average speed • see speed, average

balance (BA-lens) • a basic tool used to measure weight, 11

basic tool (BAY-sik TOOL) • a simple tool, 11

battery (BA-tuh-ree) • an object that stores chemical energy, 34-35, 66

carbohydrate (car-boe-HYE-drate) • a molecule used by the body for energy, 25, 26, 65-66

charge (CHARJ) • in physics, the ability to attract or repel, 71-72, 76, 83, 84

charge, negative (CHARJ, NE-guh-tiv) • the charge of an electron; opposite to the charge of an proton, 72, 76, 83, 84

charge, positive (CHARJ, PAH-zuh-tiv) • the charge of a proton, opposite to the charge of an electron, 72, 76, 83, 84

chemical energy • see energy, chemical

chemical reaction (KE-muh-kul ree-ACK-shun) • occurs when atoms or molecules join together, leave a molecule, or switch places, 25, 63-64, 66, 69, 70

chemical stored energy • see energy, chemical stored

coal • a source of energy that comes from the Earth, 35-36

computer (kum-PYOO-tur) • an electronic device that can store, retrieve, and process data, 13

conduct (kun-DUCT) • in physics, to allow the movement of electrons, 76, 78-80

conductor (kun-DUCK-tər) • in physics, a material that allows electrons to flow through it, 78

convert (kun-VERT) • to change from one form to another, 27, 32-36, 55-56, 69

detail (DEE-tail) • a small, particular part of a thing, 11, 48

dynamic (dye-NA-mik) **testing machine** • an advanced tool used to test the properties of objects and materials, 12

elastic stored energy • see energy, elastic stored

electrical energy • see energy, electrical

electrical (i-LEK-trik-ul) **force** • the force that causes electrons to move, 72-73

electricity (i-lek-TRI-suh-tee) • energy that comes from the flow of electrons; electrical energy, 12, 69-73, 76-80 electron (i-LEK-tron) • one of the 3 basic parts of an atom; found on the outside of the atom; has a negative charge, 69-73, 76-80, 83, 84, 86-88

energy (EN-ur-jee) • something that gives something else the ability to do work, 9, 18, 20-21, 24-28, 31-36, 62-66, 69, 70

energy, chemical (EN-ur-jee, KE-mi-kul) • energy produced by chemical reactions, 26, 31-36, 63-66, 69

energy, chemical stored (EN-ur-jee KE-mi-kul STAWRD) • stored energy that is released by chemical reactions, 25, 26, 63-66

energy, elastic stored (EN-ur-jee, i-LAS-tik STAWRD) • energy that is found in objects that are stretched, 26

energy, electrical (EN-ur-jee, i-LEK-trik-ul) • energy that comes from the flow of electrons; electricity, 66, 69-73, 77

energy, gravitational stored (EN-ur-jee, gra-vuh-TAY-shuh-nul STAWRD) • energy stored in objects that are elevated above the ground and can be pulled down by gravity, 26

energy, kinetic (EN-ur-jee, ki-NE-tik) • energy found in moving objects, 27-28

energy, mechanical (EN-ur-jee, mi-KA-ni-kul) • energy having to do with the motion or position of an object, 32

energy, nuclear (EN-ur-jee, NOO-klee-ur) • energy that comes from plutonium atoms, 35

energy, stored (EN-ur-jee, STAWRD) • energy that has not been used, 24-28, 31, 63-66

force • any action that changes the location of an object, the shape of an object, or how fast or slowly an object is moving, 18-21, 31, 39, 42-43, 62-63, 72-73, 84, 88

fossil (FAH-sul) • extremely old remains of a plant or animal that has been left in Earth's crust, 35-36

friction (FRIK-shun) • a force that causes moving objects to slow down and stop, 42-43

Galileo [Galileo Galilei (ga-luh-LAY-oh gal-uh-LAY)] • [1564-1642 CE] Italian scientist; studied motion, 4, 39

gasoline (GAS-uh-leen) • a source of energy that comes from the Earth, 32, 33, 35, 36, 64-65

gear • a simple machine that uses rotational motion, 32, 56-58

gravitational stored energy • see energy, gravitational stored

gravity (GRA-vuh-tee) • the force that holds everything to Earth's surface, 5, 26

Ibn al Haytham • [965-1040 CE] Muslim philosopher; studied light and how light rays travel, 10 inertia (i-NER-shuh) • the tendency of an object to resist a change in motion, 39-43, 62

insulator (IN-suh-lay-tur) • a material that does not allow electrons to flow through it, 80

iron • a metal that can be magnetic, 84

Khayyam, Omar (kye-YAM, OH-mar) • [1048-1131 CE] Persian scientist; accurately calculated the length of a year, 10

kinetic energy • see energy, kinetic

linear motion • see motion, linear

magnet (MAG-net) • a type of material that creates an attractive force but is not charged, 83-88

magnetic (mag-NE-tik) force • the force created by a magnet that causes it to attract or repel, 88

magnetic (mag-NE-tik) pole • one of the two opposite ends of a magnet, 84-88

mass • in simple terms, how heavy an object is, 41-42, 62

mechanical energy • see energy, mechanical

motion, linear (MOE-shun, LI-nee-ur) • motion that occurs along a line, 46-49, 53-56

motion, nonlinear (MOE-shun, non-LI-nee-ur) • motion of an object that moves in a curve or circle, 53-58

motion, rotational (MOH-shun, roh-TAY-shuh-nul) • the type of nonlinear motion of an object moving in a circle around a central point, 55-56

natural gas • a source of energy that comes from the Earth, 35-36

negative charge • see charge, negative

neutral (NOO-trul) • in physics, having no charge, 71

neutron (NOO-tron) • one of the 3 basic parts of an atom; found in the center of the atom; does not have a charge, 70, 71

nickel • a metal that can be magnetic, 84

nonlinear motion • see motion, nonlinear

north pole • in physics, one end of a magnet, 87-88

nuclear energy • see energy, nuclear

observation (ahb-sur-VAY-shun) • the act of noticing a fact about something, 6

opposite (AH-puh-zit) • on different ends or sides, 72, 83-84, 86-88

oscilloscope (ah-SILL-uh-skope) • a tool used to measure electrical waves, 12

physicist (FI-zuh-sist) • a scientist who studies physics, 3-4

physics (FI-ziks) • the branch of science the explores how the natural world works, 2-3

plutonium (ploo-TOE-nee-um) • an element used to create nuclear energy, 35

positive charge • see charge, positive

proton (PRO-tahn) • one of the 3 basic parts of an atom; found in the center of the atom; has a positive charge, 70-72

relative (REL-uh-tiv) • in comparison to something else, 47, 53

robot (ROE-bot) • a machine that can perform complicated tasks, 13

rotate (ROE-tate) • to move around a central point, 55

rotational motion • see motion, rotational

ruler • a basic tool used for making measurements, 11

Shen Kuo (SHEN GWOE) • [1031-1095 CE] Chinese philosopher; described the magnetic needle compass, 10

sound meter • a tool used to measure high and low sounds, 11

south pole • in physics, one end of a magnet, 87-88

speed • how fast an object moves, 47-49

speed, average • a value arrived at by adding together a set of measurements of speed and then dividing by how many measurements there are, 48-49

sprocket (SPRAH-ket) • a wheel that has teeth on the edge, 56-58

stored energy • see energy, stored

Thales of Miletus (THAY-leez of mye-LEE-tus) • [625-545 B.C.E.] Greek philosopher; traveled to Egypt to study geometry and astronomy, 9

thermal imager (THUR-mul IM-i-jur) • a tool used to measure small changes in temperature, 12

thermometer (ther-MOM-uh-tur) • a basic tool used to measure temperature, 11

timer • a basic tool used to keep track of time, 11

work • in physics, an event that occurs when a force moves an object, 18, 19-21, 26-28, 31, 63-64

More REAL SCIENCE-4-KIDS Books
by Rebecca W. Keller, PhD

Building Blocks Series yearlong study program — each Student Textbook has accompanying Laboratory Notebook, Teacher's Manual, Lesson Plan, Study Notebook, Quizzes, and Graphics Package

Exploring the Building Blocks of Science Book K (Activity Book)
Exploring the Building Blocks of Science Book 1
Exploring the Building Blocks of Science Book 2
Exploring the Building Blocks of Science Book 3
Exploring the Building Blocks of Science Book 4
Exploring the Building Blocks of Science Book 5
Exploring the Building Blocks of Science Book 6
Exploring the Building Blocks of Science Book 7
Exploring the Building Blocks of Science Book 8

Focus Series unit study program — each title has a Student Textbook with accompanying Laboratory Notebook, Teacher's Manual, Lesson Plan, Study Notebook, Quizzes, and Graphics Package

Focus On Elementary Chemistry
Focus On Elementary Biology
Focus On Elementary Physics
Focus On Elementary Geology
Focus On Elementary Astronomy

Focus On Middle School Chemistry
Focus On Middle School Biology
Focus On Middle School Physics
Focus On Middle School Geology
Focus On Middle School Astronomy

Focus On High School Chemistry

Super Simple Science Experiments

21 Super Simple Chemistry Experiments
21 Super Simple Biology Experiments
21 Super Simple Physics Experiments
21 Super Simple Geology Experiments
21 Super Simple Astronomy Experiments
101 Super Simple Science Experiments

Note: A few titles may still be in production.

Gravitas Publications Inc.
www.gravitaspublications.com
www.realscience4kids.com

CPSIA information can be obtained
at www.ICGtesting.com
Printed in the USA
BVHW021910040720
582961BV00004B/97